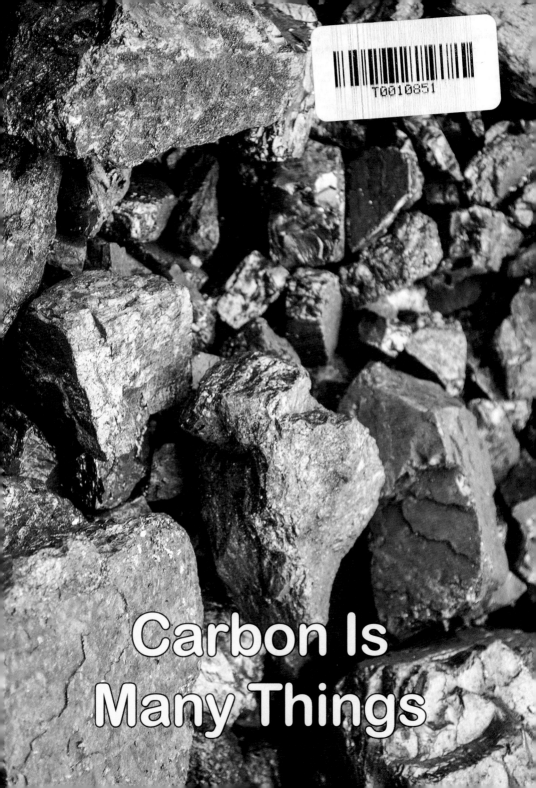

Carbon Is
Many Things

This white diamond is carbon.

This **pink** diamond is carbon.

This yellow diamond is carbon.

This blue diamond is carbon.

This black lead is carbon.

This black oil is carbon.

This black coal is carbon.

This black charcoal is carbon.